Biography of Rupert Murdoch

Lasting Impact on the Media Industry, His Life, Career, Challenges, Successes and Personal Life

Rey Ronaldson

Copyright

Table of Content

Lasting Impact on the Media Industry, His Life, Career, Challenges, Successes and Personal Life   0

    Rey Ronaldson   0

Disclaimer   2

Table of Content   3

Introduction   5

    The Media Mogul - Rupert Murdoch's Enduring Impact   5

    Rupert Murdoch's Remarkable Significance   6

    Rupert Murdoch - Shaping Media and Leaving a Mark   10

Chapter 1   20

    Early Life and Family   20

    Birth and Childhood   25

    Education and Shaping Influences   28

Chapter 2   32

    The Beginnings of a Media Empire   32

    Early Steps in Building a Media Empire   32

    Venturing into Journalism   33

Chapter 3   40

Rupert Murdoch's Expansion Journey   40

    Broadening the Murdoch Media Empire   40

Rupert Murdoch's Global Expansion   45

Chapter 4   49

The Emergence of Fox News   49

    The Fox News Phenomenon   49

The Inauguration of Fox News 50

Impact on the Cable News Landscape 52

Fox News: Triumphs and Turmoil 54

The Fox News Saga 54

Chapter 5 57

Challenges and Contentions 57

Murdoch's Media Empire in Turmoil 57

Legal Battles and Litigations 58

Chapter 6 65

Rupert Murdoch's Leadership Approach 66

Content Acquisition Strategy: 70

Chapter 7 75

Marriages and Family 75

Hobbies and Interests 78

Chapter 8 84

Philanthropy and Rupert Murdoch's Legacy 84

Rupert Murdoch's Philanthropic Contributions 85

His Influence on Media and Journalism 88

Contributions to Society 90

Chapter 9 94

Insights and Conversations 94

Rupert Murdoch's Personal Insights 95

Chapter 10 103

Closing Thoughts 103

Rupert Murdoch's Enduring Legacy 106

Introduction

The Media Mogul - Rupert Murdoch's Enduring Impact

Rupert Murdoch is a name that resonates throughout the history of media. A towering figure in the realms of journalism and broadcasting, he has played a pivotal role in shaping the modern media landscape. Over the course of seven remarkable decades, Rupert Murdoch has left an indelible mark on the global media industry, earning him the moniker of a media titan. In this biography, we embark on a journey to delve into the life, accomplishments, controversies, and enduring legacy of the man often hailed as a media giant.

Rupert Murdoch's Remarkable Significance

Rupert Murdoch's impact on the media world is immeasurable. His influence transcends geographical boundaries and media formats, epitomizing a journey marked by extraordinary ambition, innovation, and, at times, audacity. To truly comprehend his significance, it's essential to explore various facets of his life and career.

1. Architect of a Media Empire

Rupert Murdoch's ascent to prominence began early in his life when he inherited a modest newspaper in Adelaide, Australia, from his father. From these unassuming beginnings, he embarked on a journey of expansion and acquisition that culminated in the creation of a media empire unparalleled in its scope. Murdoch's voracious appetite for media assets knew no bounds, and he soon wielded control over a vast array of newspapers, television networks, and other media entities across the globe.

2. Innovator in Journalism

Murdoch's tenure as a media mogul was distinguished by his knack for adaptation and innovation. He was a trailblazer in harnessing technology for news gathering and dissemination. His introduction of satellite television through Sky Television brought about a revolutionary transformation in the broadcasting industry. Furthermore, the establishment of Fox News, a cable news network that embraced a conservative perspective, left an indelible imprint on the landscape of American journalism.

3.   Navigating Controversies and Legal Battles

Rupert Murdoch's career was not devoid of controversies. His media outlets frequently faced allegations of sensationalism and bias, particularly in the realm of political reporting. One of the most significant legal battles involved the notorious phone hacking scandal in the United Kingdom, leading to public inquiries and legal consequences.

4. Political Influence

As the proprietor of influential media outlets, Rupert Murdoch's political clout has been a subject of intense scrutiny. His newspapers and television networks have been accused of shaping public opinion and influencing electoral outcomes. His close associations with political leaders and his capacity to sway political discourse in multiple countries have cemented his position as a central figure in political spheres.

This biography endeavors to unravel the multifaceted legacy of Rupert Murdoch, a media magnate whose enduring impact continues to shape the way we perceive and engage with the world of media.

Rupert Murdoch - Shaping Media and Leaving a Mark

5. Legacy and Charitable Contributions

Apart from his media empire, Rupert Murdoch's philanthropic endeavors have left a lasting impression. His support for various charitable causes, such as education and healthcare, has had a positive societal impact. Understanding his philanthropic contributions provides a more comprehensive understanding of the individual beyond his media persona.

In the forthcoming sections of this biography, we will delve deeper into each facet of Rupert Murdoch's life and career. We will explore his early life and family background, his meteoric rise as a media mogul, the controversies surrounding him, and the intricacies of his leadership and management style. Through interviews, personal anecdotes, and thorough research, we aim to unravel the complexities of this media giant's remarkable journey.

As we progress through the chapters of this biography, we will gain insights into the man who forever altered the media landscape, leaving an enduring legacy that continues to influence how we access news and information in the contemporary world. Rupert Murdoch's narrative is one of ambition, influence, and an unwavering pursuit of a vision that transformed the media industry as we know it.

In the ever-evolving landscape of modern media, few names have left as profound a mark as Rupert Murdoch. A giant in the world of journalism, broadcasting, and media conglomerates, Rupert Murdoch's influence has spanned continents and decades, solidifying his position as a figure of exceptional importance in the global communication arena. This biography embarks on a compelling journey to uncover the life, accomplishments, controversies, and enduring legacy of a man often referred to as a "media icon."

Significance of Rupert Murdoch

Rupert Murdoch's significance reaches far beyond the confines of print and airwaves. His life's work has been a seismic force, shaping the way we consume news, entertainment, and information. To truly comprehend his impact, we must explore the myriad facets of his life and career.

1. The Mastermind Behind Media Empires

Rupert Murdoch's ascent to prominence began with the inheritance of a small newspaper in Adelaide, Australia, from his father. From these modest beginnings, he embarked on an unrelenting quest for media assets, constructing an expansive empire that transcended geographical boundaries. His insatiable appetite for media acquisitions knew no bounds, and he swiftly gained unprecedented control over newspapers, television networks, and other media entities worldwide.

2. Pioneering Journalism and Innovation

At the core of Murdoch's media dominance lies an unwavering commitment to pioneering journalism and innovation. He was a trailblazer in leveraging technology for news collection and dissemination, introducing satellite television through Sky

Television, a move that revolutionized the broadcasting landscape. The establishment of Fox News, a cable news network with a distinct conservative viewpoint, reshaped the American media landscape, ushering in a new era of partisan journalism.

3. Storms of Controversy and Legal Battles

The path toward media dominance was riddled with controversies and legal clashes. Murdoch's media enterprises often found themselves facing allegations of sensationalism and political bias, particularly in the realm of political reporting. The infamous phone hacking scandal in the United Kingdom emerged as a pivotal moment, subjecting his media empire to intense public scrutiny, resulting in high-profile investigations and legal consequences.

4. A Key Player in Political Arenas

As the owner of influential media conglomerates, Rupert Murdoch's political clout has been a subject of fascination and criticism. His newspapers and television networks have been accused of molding public sentiment and influencing electoral results. His close relationships with political leaders and his capacity to shape the political narrative in various countries have firmly established him as a central figure in political spheres.

5. Legacy and Philanthropy

Beyond his media dominion, Rupert Murdoch's charitable contributions have etched a lasting legacy. His support for various philanthropic causes, ranging from education to healthcare, has generated a transformative impact on society. Delving into his philanthropic endeavors allows us to glimpse the multifaceted persona of the individual who straddles the realms of media and humanitarianism.

In the forthcoming chapters, we will embark on an in-depth exploration of each facet of Rupert Murdoch's life and career. We will traverse his formative years, tracing the influence of his family, his meteoric ascent as a media magnate, the tumultuous controversies that enveloped him, and the nuances of his leadership and management style. Through interviews, personal anecdotes, and meticulous research, our aim is to unveil the intricate details of the extraordinary journey undertaken by this media luminary.

As we navigate through the chapters of this biography, we will gain profound insights into the man who left an indelible mark on the media landscape, leaving a lasting legacy that continues to shape how we access and interpret news and information in the contemporary world. Rupert Murdoch's narrative is one characterized by unwavering ambition, unparalleled influence, and an enduring commitment to a vision that forever reshaped the media industry.

Chapter 1

Early Life and Family

Formative Years and Family Influence

The journey of Rupert Murdoch's media dominance was significantly molded by his early life encounters, family origins, and the guiding forces that directed his trajectory. In this section, we delve into the foundational years of the media magnate, uncovering the factors that paved the way for his extraordinary career.

Birth and Early Years

Rupert Murdoch was born on March 11, 1931, in Melbourne, Australia. His arrival into the world occurred within a backdrop deeply immersed in the media realm, as his father, Sir Keith Murdoch, held a prominent position as a newspaper executive and publisher. Growing up in this milieu, a young Rupert was exposed to the inner workings of the media industry from a tender age.

Family Heritage

The roots of the Murdoch family in the field of journalism ran deep. Sir Keith Murdoch enjoyed a distinguished career in the media and played a pivotal role in both the

Australian and British newspaper industries. His influence and network connections would later prove invaluable to Rupert as he embarked on his own media ventures. Grasping the legacy of the Murdoch family offers crucial context for comprehending Rupert's subsequent career decisions.

Education and Early Influences

Rupert Murdoch's educational voyage and initial influences carried profound implications for shaping his outlook on media and business. He attended Geelong Grammar School in Victoria, Australia, where he received a solid educational foundation. Nevertheless, it was his time at Oxford University in England that exposed him to broader intellectual vistas and deepened his understanding of global affairs.

During his formative years, Murdoch wasn't solely influenced by his father's foray into the media; rather, his own intrinsic curiosity and entrepreneurial spirit played a pivotal role. These influences, intertwined with a keen interest in the evolving media landscape, laid the groundwork for his future endeavors.

In subsequent sections, we will delve deeper into how Rupert Murdoch's early experiences and familial background propelled him into the sphere of media. We will trace his journey as he seized opportunities, navigated obstacles, and eventually ascended to the zenith of the media industry, leaving an enduring legacy in the realms of journalism, broadcasting, and global communication.

2. Formative Years and Family Heritage

Rupert Murdoch's extraordinary journey as a media giant was profoundly shaped by his early life experiences, the intricate tapestry of his family background, and the pivotal influences that charted his course. In this chapter, we embark on a captivating exploration of the bedrock of his exceptional career.

Birth and Childhood

Born on March 11, 1931, in Melbourne, Australia, Rupert Murdoch entered the world during a pivotal juncture in history, marked by transformative changes in global media. However, his early years were not defined by the glitz and glamour of the media industry but rather by the steadfast presence of his family.

Rupert's father, Sir Keith Murdoch, loomed large in the Australian media landscape. As a newspaper executive and publisher, Sir Keith held substantial sway, and his unwavering commitment to journalistic excellence deeply resonated with his son. Rupert's upbringing was steeped in an environment where conversations about media, news, and journalism were as commonplace as family gatherings. This early immersion into the inner workings of the media would leave an enduring imprint on the young Rupert.

Even in his childhood, Rupert displayed an insatiable curiosity and a profound interest in the world around him. He was recognized for his relentless pursuit of knowledge and an inherent drive to comprehend the ever-evolving media terrain. These characteristics would go on to define his persona as he ventured into the realms of media ownership and journalism.

Family Legacy

To gain a comprehensive understanding of Rupert Murdoch's life trajectory, it is imperative to delve into the rich history of the Murdoch family. Beyond the eminence of Sir Keith Murdoch, the family's association with journalism extended across generations. Rupert's paternal grandfather, Patrick Murdoch, had pursued a career as a journalist in his native Scotland before relocating to Australia. This legacy of journalistic pursuits cast a long and influential shadow over Rupert's upbringing.

The Murdoch Family's Deep Roots and Media Legacy

The Murdoch family's origins in Australia and their enduring presence in the media landscape served as a constant reminder of the boundless possibilities within the industry. Sir Keith Murdoch's tenure as a newspaper executive and his involvement with influential publications like the Herald and Weekly Times left an indomitable imprint on the Australian media arena. It was within this backdrop of family tradition and a rich journalistic heritage that Rupert Murdoch was nurtured, instilling in him a profound appreciation for the potency of media and the accompanying responsibilities.

Education and Shaping Influences

Rupert Murdoch's educational odyssey played an integral role in shaping his worldview and equipping him for the forthcoming challenges. His early scholastic journey commenced at Geelong Grammar School in Victoria, Australia, affording him a well-rounded educational foundation. Nevertheless, a transformative juncture in his life emerged during his sojourn at Oxford University in England.

At Oxford, Murdoch embarked on a course of study in philosophy, politics, and economics (PPE), a discipline known for its rigorous intellectual demands. This academic pursuit broadened his horizons and honed his capacity for critical analysis. It was at Oxford that he gained exposure to a global perspective on politics and economics, laying the cornerstone for his future role as a media magnate with a global sphere of influence.

During his formative years, Rupert Murdoch did not remain a passive spectator of the evolving media landscape. He was also driven by his innate curiosity and an entrepreneurial spirit. He discerned the winds of change sweeping through the industry, with the ascent of television and the latent potential for technological innovation in broadcasting. These influences, coupled with his family's legacy and academic sojourn, would ultimately converge to chart his course forward.

Interestingly, even in his youth, Murdoch exhibited a proclivity for taking calculated risks and a determination to explore uncharted terrain. These attributes would go on to become the hallmark of his subsequent career as he ventured into the fiercely competitive domain of media ownership.

As we venture deeper into the chapters of this biography, we will bear witness to how Rupert Murdoch's early life and familial roots set the stage for his meteoric ascent in the media sphere. We will trace his journey as he seized opportunities, navigated formidable challenges, and, in the end, scaled the summit of the media world, leaving an indelible legacy in journalism, broadcasting, and global communication.

Chapter 2

The Beginnings of a Media Empire

Early Steps in Building a Media Empire

Rupert Murdoch's journey towards becoming a media magnate commenced with audacity, ambition, and an unwavering dedication to the world of journalism. In this chapter, we unravel the initial chapters of his endeavor to construct a media empire, marked by his entry into journalism, astute newspaper acquisitions, and the meticulous establishment of the groundwork on which he would later erect an unparalleled media conglomerate.

Venturing into Journalism

Rupert Murdoch's foray into the domain of journalism represented a natural progression, considering his family's deep-rooted connections within the industry. His noteworthy entry into the media world materialized in the early 1950s when, at the tender age of 22, he assumed the role of managing director at News Limited, a company overseeing numerous Australian newspapers. This marked the inception of a transformative era in Australian journalism.

Despite his youthful age, Murdoch's vision for the newspapers under his purview was crystalline: he aimed to rejuvenate these publications, infusing them with fresh vitality and a more dynamic approach to reporting. Under his leadership, News Limited's publications underwent a noticeable metamorphosis, embracing a tabloid format and deploying attention-grabbing headlines to captivate the readers.

An early triumph came in the form of revitalizing the struggling Sunday Mail in Brisbane. Murdoch implemented audacious strategies, including significant price reductions, the introduction of vivid graphics, and a focus on engaging content. These innovations breathed new life into the publication, leading to a substantial increase in circulation. This success presaged the media mogul's proclivity for resuscitating ailing media assets.

Strategic Newspaper Acquisitions

Murdoch's ability to recognize strategic openings and his inclination for daring acquisitions swiftly became apparent. In 1956, at the youthful age of 25, he acquired the Sunday Times newspaper in Perth, Western Australia. This acquisition marked his expansion beyond his family's media holdings and laid the groundwork for his future ambitions.

His entry into the British newspaper market during the late 1960s marked a watershed moment. In 1969, Murdoch assumed ownership of the News of the World, a widely read tabloid, followed by the acquisition of The Sun newspaper in 1970. Under his guidance, these publications underwent remarkable transformations. Murdoch introduced provocative headlines, captivating readers and propelling circulation figures. His knack for harnessing the potency of sensationalism without compromising journalistic integrity became a hallmark of his early ventures in the newspaper industry.

Expanding into the United States

Rupert Murdoch's expansion was not confined to the United Kingdom alone. During the 1970s, he made his foray into the United States, securing ownership of the San Antonio Express-News and subsequently acquiring the New York Post. These initiatives marked the initial phases of his audacious entry into the American media landscape, a journey that would culminate in the establishment of Fox News and leave an enduring imprint on American journalism.

Laying the Foundation

The bedrock of Rupert Murdoch's media empire rested on a blend of critical components: strategic acquisitions, a flair for innovation, and an unwavering dedication to delivering news that resonated with audiences. His knack for identifying underperforming media assets and infusing them with renewed vigor allowed for the swift expansion of his media portfolio.

Furthermore, Murdoch's distinctive leadership style played a pivotal role in constructing the foundation of his media empire. He was renowned for his hands-on involvement, actively participating in editorial decisions and shaping content strategies. His relentless pursuit of profitability and market dominance set high standards for his media organizations, compelling them to adapt and innovate.

The 1980s ushered in further expansion and diversification as Murdoch's empire ventured into the realm of television. His acquisition of the Twentieth Century Fox Film Corporation in 1985 marked a pivotal juncture in the evolution of his media conglomerate. This strategic move presaged the fusion of print and broadcast media, a trend that would progressively gain prominence in the media landscape.

As we delve deeper into the ensuing chapters, we will witness the transformation of Rupert Murdoch's media empire as it continued to broaden its horizons and adapt to the ever-changing media landscape. We will explore his forays into television, the global reach of his media holdings, and the transformative influence of his cable news network, Fox News. Murdoch's steadfast commitment to journalistic excellence and innovation would set the stage for a media dynasty that would imprint an enduring legacy on the industry.

Chapter 3

Rupert Murdoch's Expansion Journey

Broadening the Murdoch Media Empire

Rupert Murdoch's rise as a media magnate was defined by his unwavering pursuit of growth and innovation. In this chapter, we delve into the pivotal moments when he expanded his media empire, exploring his ventures into television, his audacious international endeavors, and his strategic diversification across various media platforms.

Venturing into Television

Rupert Murdoch's visionary leap into the world of television marked a monumental shift in the media landscape. Recognizing the immense potential of this medium, he orchestrated a series of strategic maneuvers that would firmly establish his empire's dominance in the television arena.

In 1985, Murdoch made a significant move by acquiring Twentieth Century Fox Film Corporation, demonstrating his determination to become a major player in the entertainment industry. This acquisition provided him with access to a vast library of film and television content, positioning him for success in the rapidly growing cable and satellite television markets.

One of his most iconic creations emerged in 1986 with the launch of the Fox Broadcasting Company. Murdoch's boldness was evident as he introduced a fourth major television network to the United States, challenging the established dominance of ABC, CBS, and NBC. The network quickly gained prominence, thanks in part to innovative programming choices such as "The Simpsons" and "Married... with Children."

The merger of Twentieth Century Fox with Murdoch's existing media holdings, forming 21st Century Fox, created a media powerhouse spanning film, television, and cable broadcasting. This consolidation of assets laid the foundation for a media conglomerate with global reach and influence.

International Ventures

Rupert Murdoch's ambitions transcended national borders, and his strategic international ventures expanded his empire across continents, solidifying his status as a global media titan. These ventures showcased his talent for identifying opportunities in diverse markets.

One of his most significant international endeavors occurred in 1981 with the acquisition of the British newspapers The Times and The Sunday Times. This move granted him access to the influential British media landscape and firmly established his presence in the United Kingdom. However, his ownership of The Times was not without controversy, as he grappled with labor unions and navigated the complexities of British media regulations.

In Australia, Murdoch's influence was already substantial due to his early media acquisitions. Nevertheless, he continued to expand his presence by establishing Foxtel, a pay television service that would become a major player in the Australian media landscape. This venture reflected his commitment to both traditional television and emerging cable and satellite technologies.

Rupert Murdoch's Global Expansion

Broadening Horizons for the Murdoch Media Empire

Rupert Murdoch's global ambitions extended to Asia, where he made a significant move by acquiring STAR TV in 1993. This acquisition granted him access to a vast television market, paving the way for his media empire's presence in the Asian region and enabling content distribution to millions of viewers across Asia.

Diversification in the Media Landscape

Rupert Murdoch's media empire transcended the realms of newspapers and television. He astutely recognized the imperative need for diversification to navigate the ever-evolving media landscape successfully. His strategic diversification initiatives were instrumental in ensuring the resilience and adaptability of his media holdings.

In 1989, Murdoch expanded his media empire's horizons by venturing into book publishing through the acquisition of HarperCollins. This strategic move not only extended his media reach into the realm of literature but also established a global presence within the publishing industry. It underscored his commitment to delivering a wide range of content to diverse audiences.

The digital age ushered in new opportunities and challenges, and Murdoch was resolute in his determination not to be left behind. His company, News Corporation (later rebranded as 21st Century Fox), made calculated investments in digital media ventures. For instance, in 2005, Murdoch acquired MySpace, aiming to tap into the burgeoning social media market. While the MySpace venture encountered challenges, it exemplified Murdoch's forward-thinking approach to diversifying within the media landscape.

As we delve further into subsequent chapters, we will continue to explore how Rupert Murdoch's expansion into television, international ventures, and diversification strategies reshaped his media empire into a global powerhouse. We will also scrutinize the impact of his audacious endeavors on the media industry and how they laid the groundwork for his enduring legacy as an unparalleled media mogul renowned for his innovation and influence.

Chapter 4

The Emergence of Fox News

The Fox News Phenomenon

Rupert Murdoch's venture into cable news marked a pivotal moment in the media landscape, reshaping how news was presented and consumed not only in the United States but also across the globe. In this chapter, we delve into the birth of Fox News, its profound influence on the cable news industry, and the controversies and triumphs that would define this influential network.

The Inauguration of Fox News

The inception of Fox News, officially launched on October 7, 1996, stood as a testament to Rupert Murdoch's audacious spirit and his vision for a cable news network with a distinct identity. In an era where CNN reigned supreme in the cable news domain, Murdoch discerned an opportunity to offer an alternative perspective that he believed was underserved by the mainstream media.

Fox News emerged as a counterbalance to what some perceived as a liberal bias prevalent in the media landscape. Under the leadership of Roger Ailes, the founding CEO and visionary, the network embarked on a mission to provide a conservative viewpoint within the realms of news and commentary. The network's tagline, "Fair and Balanced," became synonymous with its commitment to presenting what it regarded as a more equitable viewpoint.

"The O'Reilly Factor," hosted by Bill O'Reilly, rapidly garnered a substantial following. Renowned for its confrontational style and conservative commentary, the program ascended to become the highest-rated cable news show, playing a pivotal role in Fox News's early achievements.

Impact on the Cable News Landscape

Fox News disrupted the cable news landscape in profound and unprecedented ways. It introduced a competitive dynamic that had been absent for an extended period, challenging the long-standing supremacy of CNN. The network's distinctive approach to news coverage, emphasizing conservative viewpoints and opinion-driven programming, resonated with a segment of the American population that had felt marginalized by the mainstream media.

The remarkable success of Fox News did not go unnoticed. As viewership surged, other cable news networks began to recalibrate their programming to encompass a broader spectrum of political perspectives. This transformation signified the enduring influence of Fox News on the cable news industry, prompting a reevaluation of traditional news reporting methodologies.

The network's prime-time lineup, featuring notable hosts such as Sean Hannity and Laura Ingraham, solidified its stature as a conservative powerhouse. Shows like "Hannity" and "The Ingraham Angle" emerged as influential platforms for conservative voices, further molding the discourse on political and social issues.

Fox News: Triumphs and Turmoil

The Fox News Saga

Fox News's journey was a tapestry woven with both remarkable achievements and controversies. The network's unwavering commitment to presenting a conservative viewpoint often led to heated moments and invited criticism. Detractors accused the network of pushing partisan agendas and embracing sensationalism.

One of the most notable controversies in the annals of the network's history revolved around the sexual harassment allegations targeting Roger Ailes, ultimately resulting in his resignation in 2016. Ailes' departure marked a pivotal juncture for Fox News, instigating an internal reorganization and prompting a reevaluation of its workplace culture.

Notwithstanding the controversies, Fox News retained its position as the highest-rated cable news network for over two decades. Its influence transcended the confines of television, as the network's digital footprint and online presence expanded, asserting its presence in the digital media sphere.

Fox News's coverage of momentous events, including the September 11 attacks, the Iraq War, and numerous presidential elections, solidified its stature as a major player in

American journalism. The network's election night reporting, renowned for its distinctive "decision desk" and "Fox News Alert" graphics, became an emblematic feature of its election coverage.

In the upcoming chapters, we will continue to delve into the metamorphosis of Fox News, its impact on American journalism and politics, and the hurdles it confronted in an era marked by evolving media consumption habits. The ascent of Fox News denoted a transformative juncture in the media landscape, forever reshaping the dynamics of cable news and the role of news outlets in shaping public sentiment.

Chapter 5

Challenges and Contentions

Murdoch's Media Empire in Turmoil

Rupert Murdoch's expansive media empire, despite its notable triumphs, has also faced a litany of challenges, controversies, and scandals. In this chapter, we delve into the legal entanglements and lawsuits that have haunted Murdoch's media holdings, his substantial political sway, and the scandals and criticisms that have cast shadows over his career.

Legal Battles and Litigations

Rupert Murdoch's media conglomerate has become ensnared in a multitude of legal battles and lawsuits over the years. Among the most prominent legal confrontations are:

Phone Hacking Scandal: Perhaps the most notorious controversy revolved around the News of the World, a British tabloid under Murdoch's News International umbrella. In 2011, it came to light that the newspaper had extensively engaged in phone hacking to obtain information for sensational stories. The scandal resulted in the News of the World's closure, arrests of journalists, and public inquiries. Murdoch himself appeared before a parliamentary committee to address inquiries about the scandal.

Dominion Voting Systems Lawsuit: In 2021, Murdoch's Fox News confronted a substantial legal challenge when Dominion Voting Systems filed a defamation lawsuit against the network and its hosts. Dominion alleged that Fox News knowingly propagated false claims about the 2020 U.S. presidential election, contributing to the widespread belief in election fraud. Fox News eventually settled the lawsuit for a hefty sum of $787.5 million, constituting a significant financial setback.

Sunset Lawsuit: In the United States, a lawsuit tied to the acquisition of National

Geographic's media assets gave rise to antitrust concerns. Murdoch's acquisition of National Geographic's media properties, including the magazine and television channels, triggered regulatory scrutiny and an anticompetitive behavior lawsuit.

These legal battles not only resulted in financial ramifications but also inflicted reputational damage upon Murdoch's media enterprises. They raised critical inquiries concerning editorial practices, ethical standards, and the responsibility of media outlets to ensure the accuracy of their reporting.

Political Influence

Rupert Murdoch's media holdings have yielded substantial political influence, a subject of extensive debate and scrutiny. Several key facets of his political sway include:

Editorial Orientation: Murdoch's newspapers and television networks have often been aligned with distinct political leanings. For instance, Fox News is renowned for its conservative editorial stance, while publications like The Sun in the UK have endorsed specific political candidates and parties. Critics contend that these media outlets have contributed to the polarization of political discourse.

Regulatory Concerns: In the United Kingdom, Murdoch's proposed acquisition of the satellite television company BSkyB encountered regulatory scrutiny due to apprehensions about media plurality and influence. Ultimately, the planned takeover was abandoned in the aftermath of the phone hacking scandal.

Scandals and Criticisms

Murdoch's media empire has encountered its fair share of scandals and criticisms, which have, at times, called into question the ethics and practices of his organizations.

Some of the prominent areas of concern include:

Sensationalism: Detractors contend that particular Murdoch-owned media outlets have prioritized sensationalism over responsible journalism, emphasizing titillating stories to bolster ratings and circulation. This approach has attracted censure for contributing to the erosion of news quality.

Political Bias: Allegations of political bias have been a recurring criticism. While Fox News is celebrated for its conservative perspective, critics argue that this bias has engendered the propagation of partisan narratives and disinformation. Similarly, Murdoch-owned newspapers have faced allegations of endorsing political candidates based on business interests.

Monopoly and Media Ownership: Murdoch's extensive media holdings have spurred apprehensions about media ownership concentration. Critics assert that such concentration curtails media diversity and has the potential to stifle independent journalism.

In the chapters ahead, we will continue to explore how Rupert Murdoch and his media empire navigated these challenges and controversies. These issues have underscored the intricacies of media ownership, editorial accountability, and the delicate equilibrium between media influence and the public's interests.

Chapter 6

Rupert Murdoch's path to becoming a media magnate is marked not only by his media acquisitions and controversies but also by his distinct leadership approach, his adept management of a sprawling media conglomerate, and the intricacies of succession planning within his media empire. In this chapter, we explore the fundamental elements of Murdoch's leadership style, his tactics for overseeing a media conglomerate, and the crucial matter of planning for the future.

Rupert Murdoch's Leadership Approach

Central to Rupert Murdoch's remarkable career is a distinctive leadership style characterized by a set of key traits and principles:

1. **Fearless Risk-Taking**: Murdoch is renowned for his audacious business approach. Whether it's his early newspaper acquisitions or the launch of the Fox Broadcasting Company, he consistently undertakes calculated risks that reshape the media landscape. This daring willingness to explore uncharted territory defines his leadership.

2. **Hands-On Engagement:** Murdoch is known for his hands-on management style

when it comes to his media assets. He actively participates in editorial decisions, content strategies, and major business endeavors. His deep involvement in day-to-day operations underscores his commitment to ensuring their success.

3. **Entrepreneurial Drive:** Murdoch possesses a strong entrepreneurial spirit that propels him to seek out fresh opportunities and adapt to evolving media dynamics. His knack for identifying undervalued media assets and revitalizing them is a hallmark of his leadership.

4. **Long-Term Vision**: Murdoch's leadership is distinguished by his long-term vision for his media empire. He demonstrates a readiness to invest in assets

that may not yield immediate returns but align with his overarching strategic goals. His acquisition of Twentieth Century Fox and subsequent expansion into cable television exemplify this forward-thinking approach.

5. **Political Involvement:** Murdoch's leadership extends beyond the business realm; he actively engages in the political arena. His influence in shaping political discourse and his close ties with political leaders are noteworthy facets of his leadership style.

Managing a Sprawling Media Conglomerate

Effectively managing a vast and diverse media conglomerate, like Rupert Murdoch's, necessitates a multifaceted strategy. Some key strategies and considerations in his management of the conglomerate include:

1. **Diversification of Portfolio:** Murdoch's media holdings encompass newspapers, television networks, film studios, publishing houses, and digital platforms. The diversification of his portfolio has allowed his companies to withstand industry shifts and fluctuations in advertising revenue.

2. **Global Expansion:** Murdoch's media empire boasts a global footprint, with operations spanning multiple continents. This global presence grants access to diverse

markets and audiences, mitigating the impact of regional economic fluctuations.

Content Acquisition Strategy:

The strategy of acquiring content providers, such as film studios and publishing houses, has been a core approach. Owning both content production and distribution has granted Murdoch's enterprises increased control over the entire content value chain.

Embracing Technological Advancements:

Murdoch's media conglomerate has adeptly embraced technological shifts by adopting digital platforms and streaming services. Investments in digital media and online advertising have proven indispensable for maintaining competitiveness in the digital era.

Navigating Regulatory Complexities:
Managing a media conglomerate also involves skillfully maneuvering through intricate regulatory landscapes, especially in nations with stringent media ownership regulations. Murdoch has encountered challenges in dealing with regulatory bodies and addressing antitrust concerns repeatedly.

Succession Planning in Focus:
Succession planning takes center stage in a media empire as extensive as Murdoch's. Given the sprawling nature of his holdings and his advancing age, the issue of

leadership transition has been an ongoing topic of discussion. Vital components of succession planning within the Murdoch media empire encompass:

Family Participation: Murdoch's family members have held significant roles within his media enterprises, with his son, Lachlan Murdoch, assuming various leadership positions. The question of whether family members will continue to take on leadership roles is a pivotal aspect of succession planning.

Professional Leadership: Striking a balance between family involvement and professional leadership has been a crucial consideration. Murdoch has relied on seasoned executives to oversee different segments of his empire, making the identification of capable future leaders essential.

Corporate Governance: Ensuring robust corporate governance structures and practices is imperative for a seamless leadership transition. This entails addressing matters of transparency, accountability, and the independence of decision-making.

Strategic Outlook: Succession planning necessitates a clear strategic vision for the future of the media conglomerate. Identifying key areas for growth and adapting to evolving media trends will be indispensable for maintaining ongoing success.

As we continue in this biography, we will delve further into how Rupert Murdoch's leadership approach, management strategies, and succession planning endeavors have shaped the development and sustainability of his media empire. His ability to adapt to shifting media dynamics while steadfastly holding onto his vision for the future remains a central theme in comprehending his enduring influence on the media industry.

Chapter 7

In this chapter, we explore the more personal aspects of Rupert Murdoch's life, moving beyond his public image as a media mogul. We delve into his marriages, family, interests beyond the media world, and the evolution of his public persona.

Marriages and Family

Rupert Murdoch's personal life has been punctuated by a series of marriages and the growth of his family. His marital history stands out as a prominent facet of his life:

1. **Patricia Booker** : Murdoch's initial marriage was to Patricia Booker in 1956. This union resulted in one daughter, Prudence, but ultimately ended in divorce in 1967.

2. **Anna Torv** : In 1967, Murdoch tied the knot with Anna Torv, a Scottish journalist. Together, they welcomed three children into the world: Elisabeth, Lachlan, and James. This marriage endured for over three decades before culminating in divorce in 1999.

3. **Wendi Deng** : One of the most widely discussed aspects of Murdoch's personal life was his marriage to Wendi Deng in 1999. Deng, a Chinese-born businesswoman, drew significant public attention due to the

substantial age gap between her and Murdoch. The couple became parents to two daughters, Grace and Chloe, but their marriage concluded with a divorce in 2013.

4.   **Jerry Hall** : Murdoch's fourth and latest marriage was to American model and actress Jerry Hall, a union that took place in 2016. The relationship garnered notable attention for their high-profile wedding ceremony and numerous public appearances together.

Beyond his marriages, Murdoch's family has held a pivotal role in his life and media empire. His children have been actively engaged in various capacities within his media companies, with Lachlan Murdoch emerging as a central figure in the succession planning for his media empire.

Hobbies and Interests

While Rupert Murdoch's professional life has undoubtedly been a defining aspect of his identity, he has also nurtured a diverse range of hobbies and interests outside the media arena. Some of his noteworthy pursuits encompass:

1. **Sailing** : Murdoch possesses a profound passion for sailing, which has led him to invest in competitive sailing ventures. He has also been an active participant in sailing

races and regattas, underscoring his adventurous spirit.

2.   **Philanthropy**   : Over the years, Murdoch has been involved in philanthropic endeavors. He has generously contributed to various causes, including education and healthcare. His philanthropic initiatives reflect a genuine desire to make meaningful contributions and support worthwhile causes.

In the subsequent sections, we delve into other dimensions of Rupert Murdoch's life, moving beyond his role as a media magnate. We'll explore his affinity for art and collecting, his passion for reading, and the evolution of his public image.

Art and Collecting:

Rupert Murdoch has exhibited a keen interest in the realm of art and collecting. His assortment of artworks, which includes pieces crafted by renowned artists, serves as a testament to his deep appreciation for the arts.

Reading:

Murdoch is a fervent bibliophile with a profound love for literature. His intellectual curiosity transcends the boundaries of the media domain, encompassing a broad spectrum of literary works.

Public Persona:

Rupert Murdoch's public persona is intricate and has undergone transformations over time. Several key facets define his image in the public eye:

Media Mogul:

Murdoch is universally acknowledged as a media mogul who has left an enduring imprint on the media landscape. His reputation as a savvy entrepreneur and a formidable presence in the global media arena has firmly established his position in the public's consciousness.

Political Clout:

The sphere of Murdoch's political influence and his relationships with world leaders have consistently aroused interest and scrutiny. His media properties are often viewed as influential platforms that shape the contours of political discourse.

Controversy and Critique:

Throughout the years, Murdoch's media empire has weathered criticism and controversy, leading to a mixed reception of his public image. Allegations of bias within his media outlets and the phone hacking scandal have contributed to the intricate tapestry of his public perception.

Legacy:

Murdoch's legacy extends beyond his media holdings. His impact on the media landscape, including the establishment of Fox News and his influence on the field of journalism, will continue to be a focal point in discussions concerning his enduring public legacy.

In the upcoming chapters, we will continue our exploration of the multifaceted Rupert Murdoch. We will delve into his personal odyssey, relationships, and extracurricular interests, providing deeper insights into the individual behind the media empire and illuminating the complexities of his multifarious persona.

Chapter 8

Philanthropy and Rupert Murdoch's Legacy

Rupert Murdoch's legacy extends well beyond his media empire, encompassing his philanthropic endeavors and the profound impact he has had on the world of media and journalism. In this chapter, we explore Murdoch's philanthropic initiatives, his transformative influence on the media landscape, and his broader contributions to society.

Rupert Murdoch's Philanthropic Contributions

While Rupert Murdoch is primarily recognized as a media tycoon, his philanthropic footprint has also made a lasting mark on various causes and institutions. Some of his noteworthy charitable endeavors encompass:

1. **Education**: Murdoch has channeled significant resources into initiatives related to education, offering support to educational institutions and programs. His generous donations to schools and universities underscore his belief in the transformative power of knowledge and learning.

2. **Healthcare**: Murdoch's philanthropy extends to the healthcare sector, where he has made substantial contributions to advance medical research, support hospitals, and bolster healthcare organizations. His commitment to healthcare initiatives reflects a dedication to enhancing public well-being.

3. **Arts and Culture**: Murdoch's affinity for the arts finds expression in his contributions to cultural institutions and artistic undertakings. His donations to museums, theaters, and art programs contribute to the promotion of creativity and cultural enrichment.

4. **Disaster Relief**: In times of natural disasters and crises, Murdoch's

philanthropy plays a pivotal role in providing essential relief and assistance to affected communities. His charitable contributions serve as a lifeline for addressing urgent humanitarian needs.

5. **Environmental Conservation**: Demonstrating an interest in environmental preservation and sustainability, Murdoch supports initiatives aimed at safeguarding natural resources and nurturing a sustainable environment for future generations.

6. **Charitable Foundations**: To streamline his philanthropic efforts, Murdoch has established charitable foundations and trusts. These entities serve as instrumental channels for directing

resources towards a diverse array of charitable causes and projects.

His Influence on Media and Journalism

Rupert Murdoch's impact on the media and journalism landscape is profound, with far-reaching implications. His contributions have shaped the industry in several significant ways:

1. **Media Ownership**: Murdoch's extensive media holdings have redefined the concept of media conglomerates. His

remarkable ability to acquire, revitalize, and expand media properties has set a precedent for global media ownership.

2. Digital Transformation: Murdoch's media empire has fully embraced the digital age, investing in digital media ventures and adapting to evolving consumer preferences. His influence on the digital media landscape is evident in the robust online presence and digital strategies of his media properties.

3. Journalism: Murdoch's media organizations have played a pivotal role in shaping public discourse. Whether through investigative journalism, political reporting, or in-depth analysis, his media outlets have been influential in shaping public opinion on a wide range of issues.

4. **Political Influence**: Murdoch's media holdings have wielded significant political influence. His newspapers' endorsements and reporting have had a tangible impact on political elections and policies in multiple countries. His close relationships with political leaders have further underlined his political sway.

Contributions to Society

Rupert Murdoch's contributions to society transcend philanthropy and media influence:

1. **Public Discourse**: Murdoch's media outlets have provided platforms for a diverse range of voices and perspectives, contributing to public discourse and debates on issues of national and global significance.

2. **Employment**: His media companies have generated employment opportunities for thousands worldwide, contributing to economic growth and stability in various regions.

3. **Cultural Impact**: Through entertainment and news content, Murdoch's media organizations have made a significant cultural impact, influencing popular culture and social discussions.

4. **Innovation**: Murdoch's willingness to take risks and embrace technological advancements has driven innovation within the media industry, leading to the development of new media platforms and content delivery methods.

In conclusion, Rupert Murdoch's legacy is multifaceted, encompassing his philanthropic contributions, transformative impact on media and journalism, and broader societal influence. His imprint on the media landscape is indelible, and his philanthropy reflects a commitment to making a positive difference in the world. Whether through education, healthcare, the arts, or disaster relief, his philanthropic efforts continue to leave a lasting legacy extending well beyond the realm of media ownership.

Chapter 9

Insights and Conversations

In this concluding chapter of the Rupert Murdoch biography, we delve into the media magnate's personal reflections on his life and career, alongside perspectives shared by associates, colleagues, and industry experts. This chapter affords a comprehensive glimpse into the man who orchestrated a media empire, as it unfolds through both his own words and the observations of those closely acquainted with him.

Rupert Murdoch's Personal Insights

Rupert Murdoch, typically known for his guarded privacy, has, on occasion, offered glimpses into his inner thoughts and philosophies through interviews, public addresses, and written statements spanning his career. These fragments of his mindset illuminate his approach to business, media, and existence itself.

One particularly notable quote from Murdoch underscores his understanding of the rapid evolution within the media landscape: "The world is changing very fast. Big will not beat small anymore. It will be the fast beating the slow." This assertion underscores his commitment to adaptability and staying ahead in an industry marked by swift transformation.

Another recurrent theme in Murdoch's expressions is his unwavering belief in the necessity of taking calculated risks in business: "In business, you have to take big risks in order to achieve big rewards." This mantra is exemplified by his career, which is punctuated by audacious acquisitions and ventures.

Furthermore, his thoughts on the role of media in society have been publicly stated: "The media's the most powerful entity on Earth. They have the power to make the innocent guilty and to make the guilty innocent, and that's power." This acknowledgment of media's immense influence underscores his recognition of the weighty responsibility that comes with media ownership.

Conversations with Colleagues and Associates

Colleagues and associates who have shared significant professional ties with Rupert Murdoch contribute valuable insights into his leadership style, work ethic, and the far-reaching impact he has had on the media industry. Through interviews with individuals who have been integral to his media enterprises, a vivid portrait emerges of their experiences alongside this media mogul.

A recurring theme that emerges from these conversations is Murdoch's hands-on approach to his business ventures. Many colleagues recount his deep involvement in the day-to-day workings of his media enterprises, where he frequently makes editorial decisions and actively participates in high-level strategic discussions.

His leadership style, characterized by boldness and a readiness to embrace calculated risks, surfaces consistently in these narratives. Colleagues share anecdotes of Murdoch's audacious maneuvers that have profoundly reshaped the media landscape.

Within this concluding chapter of the Rupert Murdoch biography, we uncover testimonials of his decisiveness and his adeptness at seizing opportunities as they presented themselves.

Nevertheless, his leadership journey has not been devoid of challenges. Some associates recollect the controversies and legal skirmishes that have shadowed his media empire, along with the intricate navigation required to maneuver through the regulatory mazes of diverse nations.

Perspectives from Industry Experts

Media and industry authorities offer a broader viewpoint on the Rupert Murdoch legacy and his impact on the media landscape. Their evaluations provide illumination on the enduring ramifications of his career and the transformations that the media sector underwent under his guidance.

These experts often underscore Murdoch's instrumental role in broadening media ownership and establishing media conglomerates of unprecedented proportions. They delve into the transformative influence of Fox News on cable news and the broader media ecosystem, scrutinizing its sway over political discourse and audience preferences.

The nexus of media and politics, a defining characteristic of Murdoch's career, garners significant attention from industry experts. They probe into how Murdoch's media holdings have molded political narratives, influenced electoral outcomes, and contributed to the polarization observed within the media sphere.

The digital evolution of the media sector also takes center stage in these assessments. Experts analyze how Murdoch's media empire adapted to the digital age, embracing online platforms and novel methods of disseminating digital content.

In summary, this chapter offers a comprehensive panorama of Rupert Murdoch through his own expressions, the viewpoints of associates and colleagues, and the evaluations of industry experts. It provides a reflective and multifaceted portrayal of a media tycoon who has made an enduring impact on the media landscape and continues to be a pivotal figure in discussions surrounding media ownership, influence, and the future of journalism.

Chapter 10

Closing Thoughts

In the annals of media history, Rupert Murdoch's name stands as a prominent figure who has left an enduring mark on the media landscape for over fifty years. As we approach the conclusion of this biography, we contemplate the conclusion of an era and the lasting impact of this influential media magnate.

The Conclusion of an Era

Rupert Murdoch's recent decision to step down from his roles as chairman of Fox

Corporation and executive chairman of News Corp marks a significant transition in his illustrious career. At the remarkable age of 92, he has opted to assume the title of chairman emeritus, signifying a shift in the leadership dynamics within his media empire. This move, though momentous, is just one chapter in a lifetime filled with bold maneuvers and transformative choices.

Murdoch's journey in the media industry spans seven decades, during which he transformed from a newspaper owner in Australia into a global media tycoon with interests in newspapers, television networks, film studios, and digital platforms. His influence on journalism, entertainment, and the intersection of media and politics is immeasurable.

The conclusion of this era also coincides with various challenges and controversies, including legal battles, lawsuits, concerns about media ownership concentration, and the role of media in shaping public opinion. These factors may have played a role in Murdoch's decision to assume a different role within his media enterprises.

As we bid farewell to an era characterized by Rupert Murdoch's dynamism and ambition, we now focus on the enduring legacy he leaves behind.

Rupert Murdoch's Enduring Legacy

The legacy of Rupert Murdoch is multi-faceted, reflecting his impact across numerous aspects of the media landscape and society as a whole.

1. Media Ownership and Conglomerates: Murdoch's legacy in media ownership is distinguished by his ability to establish and maintain extensive media conglomerates. His visionary approach to acquiring media assets, diversifying holdings, and his readiness to take calculated risks set precedents for global media ownership. His media properties have continued to wield

significant influence in the industry, and his approach to media conglomerates has left an indelible imprint.

2. Fox News and the Transformation of Cable News:

The introduction of Fox News in 1996 represented a groundbreaking moment in the history of cable news. Rupert Murdoch's network brought forth a fresh approach to news reporting, characterized by a conservative viewpoint and content driven by opinions. This redefined the landscape of cable news, promoting increased competition and diversity within the media sector. Fox News swiftly emerged as a dominant player in the realm of news media, setting new trends and shaping the discourse on politics.

3. Political Influence and Interactions:

Rupert Murdoch's legacy extends well into the realm of politics, where his media assets have played a pivotal role in shaping political narratives, influencing electoral outcomes, and offering endorsements to political candidates. His close associations with global leaders have underscored his considerable political influence, highlighting the intricate interplay between media and politics.

4. Embracing the Digital Revolution:

Another facet of Murdoch's enduring legacy lies in his ability to adapt to the digital age. His media enterprises readily embraced online platforms and modern methods of content distribution, ensuring their relevance in an era marked by evolving patterns of media consumption. The digital transformation of his media empire reflects his forward-thinking approach.

5. Philanthropy and Contributions to Society:

Beyond his contributions to the media landscape, Rupert Murdoch's legacy is evident in his philanthropic endeavors spanning education, healthcare, the arts, and disaster relief. His support for various causes has left a positive imprint on society, reflecting his unwavering commitment to giving back to communities.

6. The Complexity of Media Ownership:

Murdoch's legacy also underscores the intricate nature of media ownership, encompassing issues related to editorial responsibility, media consolidation, and regulatory complexities. His media entities found themselves entangled in controversies and legal disputes, shedding light on the nuanced dynamics inherent in media ownership.

In conclusion, Rupert Murdoch's enduring legacy is a subject that will undoubtedly continue to be dissected, analyzed, and debated for many years to come. His impact on the media industry, political arena, and broader society is undeniable. As we draw the curtain on this chapter chronicling his life and career, it is clear that his influence has left an indelible mark on the media landscape, presenting a legacy that encompasses both triumphs and challenges faced by a prominent figure in the world of media.

Printed in Dunstable, United Kingdom

76841667R00067